APPROACH TO SELF-MANAGEMENT

Birister Sharma

Made with ❤ on the Notion Press Platform
www.notionpress.com

Dedicated to my loving wife....

Pallabi Devi Sharma

I surrendered to you, O my Lord……

"Om Namah Shivaya"

Table of Contents

One word

Nobody can manage you in your life. Only you can manage yourself. You're the best manager of your own life.

Never allow anyone to manage your life. The moment you allow anyone to manage your life, the very moment you become his or her puppet. The puppet has no life of its own; it is always swinging by the hands of other people. It depends on others. It has no life, as well as it has no aims and goals.

What do you want in your life?

Ask yourself.

Your life is only yours; nobody has the right to control you.

Manage your own life in such a manner that you can achieve everything in your life.

You can fulfill your every dream and turn it into reality.

You can enjoy your own life.

You can build your own life. You can create your own beautiful world.

You'll get your eternal bliss and peace. You can touch the great summit of your success and glory.

1. *Love yourself*

Love yourself in such a way that you don't need anybody's love in your entire life. You're the best lover of your own life. If you love yourself truly, then you can manage your life beautifully. Forget everything, but never forget to love yourself.

Manage yourself in the following ways:

Never do anything wrong in your life.

Never engage in any bad company.

Never cultivate any bad habits.

Love your body and health; treat your body like a temple and your health like your wealth.

Maintain a balanced diet. Eat healthy and think healthy.

Always think good things in your life, because the way you think is the way you become.

Follow the mantra of 'be good, do good.'

Forget everything, but never forget to love yourself.

2. Love your beloved ones

Love your beloved ones like you love yourself. Love is the most beautiful thing in this world. Spread your love as much as you can. You'll never lose anything if you give your love to anyone. If you love anything, you can do anything for yourself and for your beloved ones. There is great power in your love. Never underestimate your love. Love is the only source that brings happiness, peace, and unity to your family. Only love can unite you and your beloved ones together.

Manage yourself in the following ways:

Give love, compassion, and respect to your beloved ones unconditionally.

But never expect anything from them in return.

Never try to control them; instead, try to convince them.

Treat them like your best friends. Help them in every situation, whether good or bad.

Try to guide them rather than punish them.

Teach them with your best examples.

Don't be too possessive of them.

Follow the simple formula: 'Live and let live.'

Love is the only source that brings happiness, peace, and unity to your family.

3. Love your work

Love is the only way to reach anywhere in your life. If you believe in your love, your love will always lead you to the path of success and glory. Therefore, love whatever work you do in your life.

Manage yourself in the following ways:

Love whatever work you do in your life.

Never hate your work. Always love your work like you love your beloved ones.

Work with heart and soul. Give your 100% effort in your work.

If you really love your work, you can focus on it completely.

If you really love your work, you'll never feel tired or bored.

Try to enjoy your work.

If you love your work, you'll do great things in your life.

If you love your work, you can create miracles in your life.

Always remember, "Work is worship."

If you believe in your love, your love will always lead you to the path of success and glory.

4. Aim high

It's well quoted that 'A man without aim is like a bird without wings.'

Think for a moment: if a bird loses its wings, how could it fly? It couldn't fly. It'll become helpless. It'll become directionless. And very soon, it'll be hunted by predators.

In the same way, think about yourself: if you have no aim in your life, how can you move ahead? You'll become helpless in your life. You'll become directionless in your life.

Do you want to become helpless and directionless in your life?

Think about it!

Manage yourself in the following ways:

Always keep your aim high.

No aim, no life. You'll become directionless.

Your aim gives you proper direction.

Your aim reminds you to commit yourself to your work.

Your aim is like your pathfinder. It'll guide you in your life.

Your aim decides your success and failure.

If you have no aim, you'll never do anything in your life.

You'll always miss the golden opportunities of your life.

Your aim makes you alert to do your work on time.

Your aim awakens you to do your work, even if you feel tired and sick.

No aim means you have no work. No work means you have no life.

No life means you have nothing.

No aim means you have no idea about yourself and your life.

A high aim means high work. High work means a higher life. A high life means happiness and success.

You have to decide for yourself.

Always keep in mind that animals have no aims and goals, but it is only man who has aims and goals.

A man without aim is like a bird without wings.

5. Make plans

Without making any plans in your life, you can't do anything properly. If you want to do anything properly in your life, you've got to make a proper plan. Your plan is the first step to initiating anything.

The soldiers never attack the enemy without making any plans. They always make plans before they attack any enemy. They know very well that if they attack the enemy without making any plans, they will commit suicide.

Manage yourself in the following ways:

Make your plans every day.

If you know how to make a plan in your life, you'll know how to live your life.

Without making any plans, you can't do anything properly in your life.

Make plans for your work.

Make plans for your family.

Make plans for your children.

Make plans for your career.

Make plans for your health insurance and life insurance.

Make plans for your wealth and prosperity.

Make short-term plans for your daily budgets, weekly budgets, and monthly budgets.

Make long-term plans for your investments and other important projects.

Don't do anything without making a plan.

If you do anything without making a plan, you'll always commit a blunder in your life.

It's only your plan that will help you achieve what you want in your life.

Never do anything without making a plan.

It's only your plan that will guarantee your success.

Your life is like a battle. If you want to win the battle of your life, you've got to make plans at every step.

Always remember that no battle is won without making a plan.

Your plan is the first step to initiate anything.

6. *Positive attitude*

No matter what happens in your life, whether you win or lose, whether you become successful or a failure, whether you smile or weep, never forget to keep your positive attitude. Your positive attitude is the only characteristic that holds you up in every harsh situation of your life.

Only your positive attitude will change the whole course of your life. If you keep your positive attitude, you'll always see success in every failure. On the other hand, if you maintain a negative attitude, you'll always see failure in every opportunity. Without a positive attitude, you can't do anything in your life. Your positive attitude is the only source of your success and glory.

Manage yourself in the following ways:

Always try to see the positive in everything.

Always keep the rays of hope.

Don't focus on your downfall and failure.

Always look at your success and glory.

Always try to upgrade yourself.

Grow and develop yourself every day.

Never look back in your life.

Always try to look for your bright future.

Prepare your mind, body, and soul for everything.

Never hesitate to take hard decisions in your life.

Learn to transform yourself according to the situation.

Your positive attitude is the only source of your success and glory.

7. Believe

You believe in yourself; that's why you're living now. But when you stop believing in yourself, the very moment you'll see your downfall. Everything will appear dark and gloomy in front of you. You'll only see unhappiness and worries everywhere.

When you start believing in yourself, the very moment you'll see your success and glory. Everything will appear colorful and beautiful in front of you. You'll only see joy and happiness everywhere.

Manage yourself in the following ways:

Always believe in yourself.

Don't fear anything in your life.

Your fear is the biggest enemy of your growth and development.

Stop self-doubting.

Come out of your comfort zone.

Keep yourself ready to face the challenges of your life.

Nothing is impossible for you.

Dare to win anything.

Make your mind strong and powerful.

Always keep the attitude of "I can do it."

You can do anything in your life.

You can achieve everything in your life.

You can win any battle in your life.

You can create anything in your life.

You can discover anything in your life.

You can invent anything in your life.

You can become a master in your field.

When you start believing in yourself, the very moment you'll see your success and glory.

8. Self-confidence

Your self-confidence is the biggest strength of your life. Without self-confidence, you can't act on anything, even if you know very well that you can act.

Your self-confidence is your inner strength. Always keep your self-confidence as your valuable asset. Never lose your self-confidence in your life.

If you lose your self-confidence, you can't think; you can't dream; you can't plan; you can't decide; you can't prepare; you can't work; you can't move; and you can't do anything in your life.

Your self-confidence is your strength and courage. Never lose it. You've to develop your self-confidence.

If you have self-confidence, nobody can stop you from becoming successful in your life.

Manage yourself in the following ways:

Your self-confidence is your inner power.

You've to develop your self-confidence inside you.

You can awaken your self-confidence when you believe in yourself.

There is tremendous power in your self-confidence.

Before you do anything, think properly and plan properly.

You should know what to do and what not to do.

Try to make the best plans.

Try to make the best decisions.

Don't proceed to do anything without making the best decisions.

Analyze your decisions and judge your decisions.

Try to prepare yourself before you initiate anything.

Don't feel tired and bored while doing your work.

Rest, but never retire.

Give up your idleness and boredom.

Keep yourself motivated and in high spirits.

Always try to see everything with a positive outlook.

21

Your self-confidence is your strength and courage.

9. Self-control

Your self-control is very significant in your life. Without self-control, you can't control your life. If you know how to control yourself, you'll know how to control others.

Your self-control decides how you can control your mind and thoughts, and how you can control your emotions and actions in your life.

Nobody can control you. Only you can control yourself.

Never allow anyone to control you. Always keep your remote control in your hands. You're the controller of your own life.

Manage yourself in the following ways:

Always control your thoughts. Don't allow them to control you.

Always control your habits. Don't allow them to control you.

Always control your actions. Don't allow them to control you.

Always control your language. Don't allow it to control you.

Always control your emotions. Don't allow them to control you.

Always control your happiness. Don't allow it to control you.

Always control your worries and tensions. Don't allow them to control you.

Always control your desires. Don't allow them to control you.

Always control your wishes. Don't allow them to control you.

Always control your wants. Don't allow them to control you.

Always control your needs. Don't allow them to control you.

Always control your love. Don't allow it to control you.

Always control your hatred. Don't allow it to control you.

Always control your anger. Don't allow it to control you.

Always control your fear. Don't allow it to control you.

Always control your greed. Don't allow it to control you.

Always control your lust. Don't allow it to control you.

Always control your jealousy. Don't allow it to control you.

You're the controller of your own life.

10. *Self-discipline*

Your self-discipline is very important for you to maintain yourself. Without your self-discipline, you can't make yourself active and punctual in your life.

It is only your self-discipline that makes you aware of everything in your day-to-day life; you'll know what to do, when to do it, and how to do it. You'll know the importance of your own life.

Without your self-discipline, you can't manage your life. Your life will always become indisciplined. You'll find yourself in a condition of unmanaged confusion and disturbances.

Your self-discipline brings complete discipline to your life.

Your self-discipline is the art of your living.

Once you know how to maintain your self-discipline, you'll know the art of living.

If you're self-disciplined, you'll always be successful in your life.

Your self-discipline is the best mantra to manage your life.

Manage yourself in the following ways:

You must be aware of everything in your life.

You must keep yourself active.

You must know your daily routine.

You must know your own duties and responsibilities.

You must keep everything ready for yourself.

You must know the importance of your time.

You must know how to manage your time for yourself and for your family members.

You must know the importance of your own health as well as your own wealth.

You must know the importance of discipline.

Once you know how to maintain your self-discipline, you'll know the art of living.

11. Be responsible

Be always responsible in your life. Whatever you do in your life, always be responsible. Never do anything without taking responsibility.

Your life is like a journey. In this journey of your life, you're like the driver of your own car. If you drive your car carefully, you'll always reach your destination safe and sound. But if you drive your car carelessly, you'll never reach your destination safe and sound.

You're responsible for everything in your life.

If you do good deeds in your life, you're responsible. If you do bad deeds in your life, you're responsible. You have to pay the price for both good deeds as well as for bad deeds.

Nobody is responsible for your life. You're responsible for both your success and failure.

If you're responsible in your life, it means you know what is right for you and what is wrong for you. You'll know the difference between the right thing and the wrong thing.

Manage yourself in the following ways:

Before you act on anything, think a hundred times.

Before you do anything, evaluate yourself.

Judge yourself before you commit to doing anything.

Calculate your own risk factors.

Never try to do anything using a shortcut method.

You should know what is right for you and what is wrong for you.

You should know when to act and when to react.

You should know what to give and what not to give.

Be your own guide as well as your own teacher.

Understand your own limitations, both your strengths and weaknesses.

Never do anything with blindfolded eyes.

Never believe in anything until you witness and experience it yourself.

Nobody is responsible for your life.

You're responsible for both your success and failure.

12. *Prepare yourself*

To do anything in your life, first of all, you've got to prepare yourself. Your preparation is the first mantra to do anything in your life. Without preparing yourself, never try to do anything in your life.

If you ever forget to prepare yourself before you do anything, your failure is one hundred percent sure. But if you prepare yourself before you do anything in your life, your success is one hundred percent sure.

You can never expect good results without preparation in your life. Your preparation is the secret of your success and glory.

Have you ever heard about anyone who has cleared any exam without preparation?

No.

It is never possible to clear any exam without preparation.

Your preparation is the secret of your success and growth in your life.

No preparation, no result. No result, no success. No success, no growth. No growth, no life. No life, nothing.

If you want to become successful in your life, then prepare yourself every day. Keep your preparation ongoing until you become an expert in your field. Your preparation is the first source of your success.

Manage yourself in the following ways:

Prepare yourself every day.

Never do anything without preparing yourself.

Always prepare yourself one hundred percent.

Full preparation means a full chance of your success.

Half preparation means a half chance of your success.

No preparation means zero chance of your success.

Prepare yourself in such a manner that you'll become a master in your chosen field.

Prepare yourself before you do anything.

Prepare yourself before you speak anything.

Prepare yourself before you work on anything.

Prepare yourself before you act on anything.

Prepare yourself before you play anything.

Prepare yourself before you create anything.

Prepare yourself before you paint anything.

Prepare yourself before you compose anything.

Prepare yourself before you write anything.

Prepare yourself before you challenge anything.

Your preparation is the first mantra for doing anything in your life.

13. Be punctual

Be always punctual in your life. As you give value to your life, in the same manner, give value to your time.

Don't delay doing anything in your life. Be always on time.

Respect your time. As you respect your time, time will respect you back. Never disrespect your time.

Don't postpone anything. If you postpone your time, time will postpone your growth and success.

If you want to become successful in your life, always be punctual in whatever you do.

If you're punctual, you'll always get whatever you want in your life.

Your punctuality is a sign of your growth and development.

Manage yourself in the following ways:

Try to become disciplined in your life.

Don't delay doing anything in your life.

Don't wait for tomorrow.

Always try to act now.

Don't miss anything in your life.

Always be ready to grab new opportunities in your life.

Never misuse your precious time.

Don't take your work as bondage.

Love your work and enjoy it.

Try to simplify your workload.

Use your intelligent mind in every task.

Try to focus only on your growth and development.

Always try to act smartly in every approach.

Your punctuality is a sign of your growth and development.

14. Don't waste time

Time is a very precious commodity for you. Always use your time for productive purposes. Don't waste your time on unproductive and unwanted things. You have only 24 hours in a day. Within this allotted time, you have to do everything in your life. Everybody has only 24 hours in a day, whether rich or poor; whether a successful person or a failure; whether a winner or a loser. Use your time only for your growth and development. Wasting time means wasting your valuable life. Your time is your life. No time, no life.

Manage yourself in the following ways:

Divide your time according to your needs and requirements.

Make your daily schedules.

Follow your timetable every day.

Learn to manage your time properly.

The way you manage your time is the way it will manage your life.

Spend your time wisely, like you spend your hard-earned money.

Don't spend your valuable time on useless stuff.

Avoid the habit of useless gossip.

Stop spending too much time watching the idiot box (television).

Spend your valuable time learning new things.

Spend your valuable time exploring new ideas.

Spend your valuable time acquiring new skills and techniques.

Spend your valuable time reading good books.

Spend your valuable time developing your personality.

Spend your valuable time creating new things.

Spend your valuable time gaining knowledge and wisdom.

Wasting time means wasting your valuable life.

15. Discover yourself

The toughest thing in your life is to discover yourself. But when you discover yourself, you'll know the beauty of your life. You'll know how to control and manage yourself. You'll learn the art of living. You'll know the meaning of your life. You'll know the purpose of your life. You'll know how valuable you are.

Everything is inside you. You just need to discover yourself. You have to look inside yourself. You'll only discover yourself when you look inside you. And once you know how to look inside you, you'll discover yourself. Everything will appear crystal clear to you.

Manage yourself in the following ways:

Think about yourself every day.

Talk to yourself every day.

Do meditation every day, both morning and evening.

Ask questions of yourself.

Try to figure out your strengths and weaknesses.

Try to figure out your skills and talents.

Find out what is good for you and what is bad for you.

Try to find out which things are naturally inclined to you.

Try to find out your good habits and bad habits.

Try to find out your likes and dislikes.

Try to find out your hobbies.

Try to review yourself every day.

You'll only discover yourself when you look inside yourself.

16. Never compare

The Sun and the Moon, the former is hot, shine on the day; and the latter is cool, shine at night. They follow different laws of the universe. They are completely different from each other. We can't compare the Sun and the Moon.

In a similar fashion, you're different from other people. Your looks are different from those of other people. Your life is different from that of other people. Your world is different from that of other people. You've nothing to do with other people.

If you ever compare yourself with other people, it means you don't know yourself. You've doubts about yourself. You feel low and inferior to other people. You're making a fool of yourself. You're neglecting yourself. You're committing a crime against yourself. You're diverting yourself from your realities. You're trying to flee from your own life. You're just inviting your failure and downfall.

Never compare yourself with other people, even if you're feeling tired, weak, helpless, and hopeless in your life; instead, focus on your own life and your own work. Comparing yourself to other people brings fear, self-doubt, anxiety, anger, greed, jealousy, and hatred into your life. You'll never gain anything from it.

Your life is only yours. You have every right to make your life purposeful and beautiful.

Manage yourself in the following ways:

Stop comparing yourself to other people.

You're unique.

Nobody is like you.

You're different from others.

Your likes are different from those of others.

Your dislikes are different from those of others.

Your thoughts are different from others.

Your dreams are different from others.

Your ideas are different from others.

Your decisions are different from others.

Your actions are different from others.

Your plans are different from others.

Your habits are different from others.

Your hobbies are different from others.

Your work is different from others.

Your lifestyles are different from others.

Your growth and development are different from others.

Never compare yourself with other people, even if you're feeling tired, weak, helpless, and hopeless in your life.

17. Be flexible

Are you always finding yourself short of time at work as well as at home? If your answer is yes, then you're not flexible in your life; and if your answer is a big no, then you're flexible in your life.

If you're flexible, you'll know how to manage yourself. You'll know your own duties and responsibilities. You'll know how to maintain your self-discipline.

If you're flexible, you'll get enough time for your work as well as for your enjoyment and entertainment.

If you're flexible, you'll always remain happy and peaceful in your life.

Manage yourself in the following ways:

Always manage yourself properly.

Manage your time properly.

Do your first thing first.

Stop procrastinating.

Make a pre-plan for your work.

Stop overdoing anything.

Always do the things that are important to you.

Don't try to do insignificant things.

Don't do anything without making proper plans.

You must know your top priority.

Clarify things for yourself before you do anything.

Learn to balance your personal life with your professional life. Don't try to combine them.

If you're flexible, you'll know how to manage yourself.

18. Accept the challenges

Always ready to face every challenge in your life. Your life is full of challenges. You're born in the midst of challenges. You're the son of challenges. The challenges of your life are nothing but a way to make you stronger and more powerful.

Don't be afraid to face the challenges of your life. Face the challenges of your life like a brave soldier.

You never get anything in your life without challenges. Make friends with the challenges of your life. Accept them gladly and hug them like your best friend.

Welcome the challenges of your life with your powerful skills, talents, courage, and high spirit.

Every challenge in your life brings you new direction and new opportunities.

If you fight against the challenges of your life, you'll always witness your grand success and glory.

Transform yourself according to the challenges of your life. If your challenges are big, then make yourself bigger and stronger than your challenges. Then no big challenges in your life will ever defeat you. You'll always come out with flying colors.

Manage yourself in the following ways:

Always prepare yourself.

Be brave and courageous.

Always keep your spirits high.

Polish your skills and talents.

Try to figure out your strengths.

Work before anything happens.

Don't wait for anything to happen.

Think first. Act first. Do first. Go first. Move first.

Believe in your own potential.

Learn to smile in the face of your downfall and failure.

Don't try to move backward; instead, try to move forward.

Try to bounce back after every hard fall.

Figure out the root causes of your challenges.

Uproot your challenges from their origin. Don't leave them.

Revenge your challenges with your mighty victory.

Welcome the challenges of your life with your powerful skills, talents, courage, and high spirit.

19. Be content

If you become the ruler of this entire universe, but you're not content with yourself, your life is meaningless. If you become the richest man in this entire world, but you're not content with yourself, your life is worthless.

Your life is not defined by how much bigger you become or how much richer you become, but by how content you are with yourself.

A monk always remains happy and content. He has nothing. He spends his life begging, but he is happy and content. He only begs for what he needs. He knows his contentment is not dependent on holding a high position or possessing huge wealth.

The biggest tragedy of a man is that he is never content with himself, even if he has a big house, a happy family, a good job, and a good bank balance.

The main reason is that he doesn't know what he wants in his life and what he needs in his life. He just wants more and more and starts running after the things that are actually not his needs, just his wants, and he himself creates the webs of his unhappiness and discontentment.

You'll find your happiness and contentment within yourself. You'll never find your happiness and contentment in the external world.

Manage yourself in the following ways:

Never expect anything from anybody.

The more you expect, the more you'll get disappointments.

Believe in your hard work.

Never try to build your castle in midair.

Be realistic and practical in your life.

Don't cross the limitations of your wants and needs.

You must know the difference between your wants and needs.

You should handle yourself according to the situation.

Don't be too materialistic in your life.

You should know how to control your emotions.

Learn to enjoy your life, both in happiness and sorrow.

Your life is always ups and downs.

Always keep a positive attitude.

Don't keep the keys to your happiness and peace in the pockets of other people.

Be the guardian of your own joy and happiness.

Follow the mantra of 'simple living and high thinking.'

Your life is not defined by how much bigger you become or how much richer you become, but by how content you are with yourself.

20. Patience

A hen lays her eggs patiently, but she doesn't smash her eggs. She keeps her patience continuously until her baby chick comes out of the eggs.

A pregnant mother carries her unborn baby in her womb for nine months while keeping her patience only to see her baby.

A sculptor keeps his patience only to create a masterpiece in his work.

Without patience, nobody can do anything.

If you grow a mango tree today, you can't get its fruit within a day, a week, or a month, but you have to wait patiently for at least 5-6 years, more or less. You can't cut down the mango tree if it doesn't give you any fruit within a few days. But you have to wait patiently for many years to get its fruits.

In a similar manner, you can't get anything within a day or a month, but you have to wait patiently for many years.

For instance, you can't learn any skill within a day, a month, or even a year, but you have to wait patiently for many years to become an expert in that skill. Many people quit too early from their work only because they can't wait patiently for the final result of their efforts. Always keep your patience until you see your grand success, no matter what happens in your life. Patience means your success and growth; impatience means your failure and downfall.

Manage yourself in the following ways:

Never hasten to do anything in your life, because haste makes waste.

Keep your mind, body, and soul in total control.

Don't do anything that other people are doing.

Do the things you love and enjoy the most.

Don't follow the paths of others.

Build your own road to success.

Learn to keep yourself busy with your work.

Stop looking for instant gratification in your life.

Learn to wait for the final result of your hard work.

Don't expect to get anything in a hurry.

Don't quit too early.

Learn to wait and watch.

You can't get anything within a day or a month, but you have to wait patiently for many years.

21. Be optimistic

If you're optimistic, you'll always remain hopeful in your life. You'll see your bright future. Your mindset will become positive. Your attitudes will be high and positive. You'll gain tremendous energy and power within yourself. You'll never quit, even if you experience downfall and failure in your life. You'll bounce back and fight against the challenges of your life.

Every successful person is optimistic. He is always hopeful in every situation of his life, whether he faces failure or defeat.

The defeated player never thinks that he won't win his next match; instead, he'll remain hopeful and believe in himself that he can defeat his opponent in the very next match. He is optimistic that he'll become a winner in his next match.

If you're optimistic, you'll always see your golden opportunity in every calamity. On the other hand, if you're pessimistic, you'll always see your failure in every opportunity.

If you're optimistic, you'll always see the beauties and wonders of your beautiful life.

If you're pessimistic, you'll always see the dark and ugly faces of your life.

If you want to become optimistic in your life, never kill your hopes, dreams, self-belief, self-confidence, self-discipline, high spirit, and energy; but always keep alive your hopes, dreams, self-belief, self-confidence, self-discipline, high spirit, and energy.

Manage yourself in the following ways:

Never give up your hopes.

Never give up your dreams.

Never give up your aims and objectives in life.

Never give up your work.

Always focus on your work.

Always keep a positive attitude.

Always keep alternative ways.

Always wait for the right time, then act.

Don't try to do anything silly.

Keep burning the midnight oil.

Believe in yourself.

Maintain your self-confidence.

Maintain your self-discipline.

Keep your spirits high and your energy up.

Always keep your patience.

If you're optimistic, you'll always see your golden opportunity in every calamity.

About the author:

Birister Sharma is a full time author. He is also an avid reader. He loves reading, writing, and motivation. He has penned down dozens of self-help motivational books and novels so far.

You may contact him @ birister2007@gmail.com